LOST
BUT MAKING GOOD TIME

poems by

Greg Moglia

Finishing Line Press
Georgetown, Kentucky

LOST
BUT MAKING GOOD TIME

Copyright © 2017 by Greg Moglia
ISBN 978-1-63534-131-7 First Edition
All rights reserved under International and Pan-American Copyright Conventions.
No part of this book may be reproduced in any manner whatsoever without written permission from the publisher, except in the case of brief quotations embodied in critical articles and reviews.

ACKNOWLEDGMENTS

Borderlands—Texas Poetry Review—"Burger Days"
Blood and Thunder—U. of Oklahoma College of Medicine—"Sexually Active"
Bryant Literary Review—"Elvis at the Dunkin Donuts"
Chiron Review—"Delios"
Connecticut River Review—"About the Lie of Divorce"
Fire (England)—"The Mill at Lowell, Mass"
Grey Sparrow Journal—"There are Skies that are Closer to the Truth"
Healing Muse (SUNY Upstate Medical U)—"Not Yet Mother Said"
Paterson Literary Review—"My Feminine Side," "Pietro and Clorinda," "Pietro's Work Shoes," "Dad and Me Fixing Things"
The New Writer (England)—"Finally a Son"
The Reader (England)—"Subway Eyes"
Shemom—"Dear Dear Family"
Southern Humanities Review—"Colic"
The Dalhousie Review (Canada)—"The Swerve"
Thema Literary Society—"Small Talk"
William and Mary Review—"In Her Bedroom"

Publisher: Leah Maines

Editor: Christen Kincaid

Cover Art: Pixaby

Author Photo: Greg Moglia

Cover Design: Elizabeth Maines

Printed in the USA on acid-free paper.
Order online: www.finishinglinepress.com
also available on amazon.com

Author inquiries and mail orders:
Finishing Line Press
P. O. Box 1626
Georgetown, Kentucky 40324
U. S. A.

Table of Contents

PART I
Finally a Son 1
Pietro and Clorinda 2
Pietro's Work Shoes 3
Colic 4
Dear Dear Family 5
Dad and Me Fixing Things 6
Not Yet Mother Said 7
Iced 8
Burger Days 9
Schenectady 10
When We Meet 11
Orbiting 12
Why Do Lovers Whisper? 13
The Swing at Orient Point 14
Love and the Bastard 15

PART II
Valentine's Day at the Home 18
About the Lie of Divorce 19
My Feminine Side 20
In Her Bedroom 21
My Red Dress 22
I Don't Know 23
Delios 24
Elvis at the Dunkin Donuts 25
Subway Eyes 26
Sexually Active 27
Small Talk 28
The Swerve 29
There are Skies that are Closer to the Truth 30
As a Kiss 31
Baffling 32

PART I

FINALLY A SON

My Dad could still do most of his own undressing
But you had to pull the T-shirt over his head

And his socks were trouble as arthritis had inflated his legs
We move snail-like to the shower and I leave him for a time

Stranded at the towel rack while I test the temperature, wet a washcloth
He reaches into the shower finds it too warm and I adjust until I hear *ok*

His body the shape of a penguin enters with a shuffle
So slippery he says, *so slippery*

I begin by soaping his back easing the cloth over and down
When I reach his butt crack he proudly announces

I'm pretty clean down there
I use the washcloth every time I take a crap

My free hand feels his skin, smooth and childlike
I soap his bald head and a circling crown of white

I rinse gently, heed his warning not to let the spray enter his ear
Facing me now, my eyes flash to his genitals, which I rush to clean quick

I need an excuse to touch this sacred ground
We need to fight rashes I say

Yes, he answers and after a final rinse
I grab a towel and begin to dry

The older you get the more like a baby he says
He shivers and I hear

I still feel cold, dry more under my arms

PIETRO AND CLORINDA

Manhattan 1920—my grandfather
A bull of a man
Strong enough to toss
An intruding salesperson
Over the hood of a Model T
Flat onto Orchard Street

Long Island 1955—now a widower
In the suburban basement
Of my boyhood home
Alone by the oil furnace
Grieving
Clorinda Clorinda he cries

I want the old man to go away
To let me live my teen years
Without this basement ghost
In his cries I see grandmother
My childhood love
Clorinda Clorinda

The hills of Tuscany
Ring with his gruff voice
The silence of angels in her eyes
The great bulk of a man
Is on his knees
Surrendering to her fingers
Moving through his hair

PIETRO'S WORK SHOES

This grandson learned about them as a six-year-old
The fifth story tenement on Mulberry Street
No hot water, little heat and here's Pietro
After his twelve hour workday...the lean tough tiger
Worn out, worn down...drops into the kitchen chair
Bends out his leg in my direction and I know what to do
Untie the knot, loosen the laces and pull
Reach under the shoe and pull, he does not help
He cannot help, his mighty arms too weary
I give a twist, then another...the shoe off...his foot free
Bravo, bambino bravo

In its time it's all natural...it's what a grandson does
But years later I think of Pietro so drained and it hits
He is not the elite worker at construction—the bricklayer
The one block at a time... done well... like artwork
No Pietro was the helper...the wheelbarrow hauler
Brick by brick, fill...carry...dump...fill...carry...dump
His work will make the day's bread a certainty

And allow him on Saturday to take me to Orchard Street
For new shoes and I will not know that their shine
Bought at the cost of the dust
On those other shoes

COLIC

This business about love—how we grow into it
The wish—to meet, share dreams, off to the castle
No, it's more like you're 12 and baby sister has the colic
Something in her stomach folds her into a knot

Mom, at the point of exhaustion hands her to me
This living twisting pain and I'm asked to take care
Me, the smart boy, good grades and not much else
Now handed the cries and curls and with them

I start around the kitchen table and the howls
Do not stop but I circle and circle hold on
And hold on until it ends but something did not end
My trips around that table became family myth

The older brother—caretaker to sis
Hearing it, I nodded yes, but unbelieving
Love to me—all honeymoon—painless and dreamy
This something else—something about sacrifice

Something about seeing
What I am made of

DEAR DEAR FAMILY

Mother opens the Van Camp baked beans
Drops the hot dogs—counts eight—into boiling water
Father at the kitchen table reading the *Times*
Defender of the working man
Has parlayed a postal clerk's salary
Into a middle class life

I, his high school son, lounge
Knees up at the same table
Head hidden behind the sport pages
Get those knees off the table Mother says
I lost in the box scores
She warns a second time

Get those feet down
Was it the sameness of her days?
Another hot dog supper
No cash for even a movie
Once more *Get those feet down*
The knife flies out of her hand

Sticks for a moment in my knee
Falls to the ground with a clatter
I told you, knees off the table she shouts
Father says *Are you crazy?*
I reach for a napkin
Limp to the bathroom

The next day mother
Unwraps the chopped chuck
Grates an onion, rolls it into the meat,
Forms a patty—counts them—eight burgers
Takes the steak knife, slits open a package
Of frozen French fries
At the table I sit upright

DAD AND ME FIXING THINGS

At the conference, a first—make the morning coffee for all fifty attendees
The coffee maker a bit different—I think no sweat but I worry
Sadly I'm my father's son—a man never seen holding a hammer Dad's
home life a quiet read of the TIMES in his easy chair

I think of the day he tried to change a storm window
He wrestles with it, falls on his bad knee just as he hears
Another of Mother's incessant complaints to do something about the boys
Something he usually brushed aside and look, me by chance nearby

He slaps me hard on the cheek and says *Obey your mother*
His one time loss of cool, he might as well have said
Avoid me when I try to do home repair
Now, a son can make a law about his father and hold tight to it

Even in the face of the unexpected
Or use the surprise to change—claim a hidden Dad lurks
Oh passive aggressive, oh Freudian, oh psychological world
And the choice comes to me even now and brings

To my cheek
No sting
Only a slow
Sweet tear

NOT YET MOTHER SAID

Don't call, not yet
Brother and mother at each side of Grandpa Pietro
He slumped, head loose on a kitchen chair
His day collecting trashed newspapers had done him in

My brother, an innocent seventeen shouts
Mom, call 911, quick
Hears *No wait, let's see if he comes out of it*
Eighty-eight years old and mother says wait

For years she cared for her father-in-law
Grumpy old man always in the way
Here, it just might end
Her home cleared of the extra table setting

When brother finally defies her and calls
It's too late, and Mother has her way
Today I ask her why?
Did you ever clean his underwear?

Cook him even one supper?
Not go on a vacation…for eight years…eight years?
I say *No mother, but you and brother Ron*
I'm pulled apart, left with an ache

ICED

At twenty-one fearless I take a front step with ease.
But Albany winter cares little for arrogant life

And ices me onto the sidewalk with a splat.
I feel a pull at my hip…almost a crack.

Know I have to stay prone for a time.
Scan a space empty of movement

Left alone with the cold seeping in
Was the slip a last twitch for me?

I get up and hobble to the corner
But I carry the alarm of the question.

Hear it again years later
When a young poet in my class

Comes to me as daughter to father
Hands me her careful words

Asking as I asked that terrified self
Tell me I am not alone

Fire my heart.

BURGER DAYS

Too many flies and mosquitoes above the burgers
And the manager had just invested
In a bug spray can the size of a fire extinguisher
So before busy time on Sunday
He asks me to fire away and I refuse
My college course in Ecology playing in my head.
He gets Eddie just out of reform school
To take my place and Eddie loves it.
Suddenly, the burger labels
Papa, Mama, Teen, and Baby
And customer toxic dose meet.

When the place begins to buzz with activity
I am too slow for the grill and shift to the fryer.
And I stay until Big Bob shows up
Lean and tall and short on talk.
An ex-con the manager said.
Big Bob tells me to step aside
Sit, relax and take care of supplies.
Big Bob did it all
Set the burgers, the rolls,
Timed the fries, ran the drinks
Wraps the deal faster than
Any four of us college guys.

I left to wonder about the world
And why it seemed so difficult?
In school even philosophy was simple
You learned that there were no answers
You told the prof as much, and you got an A.
But here the bugs land on the burgers
The best worker is an ex-con and
There are answers everywhere
And I know none of them.

SCHENECTADY

Semester break at Albany State, one beautiful week to study what I wish
Science major always experiments to do; now a chance to embrace thought
To the library for Camus, Sartre and that gigantic word
Existentialism—I learn that the world is fiercely unkind

Accident, disease, brutality—death always at the door
So since I can die at any time, to hell with tradition, with laws of my life
'Shy guy' here can dump his past and seek...seek... of course...the girl...
Before I die I'll initiate a meeting...and in my library there she is

Karen—petite, blonde, perky, the only cutie in Chem class
Hi, how about going out for an ice cream cone? Yes
Wow, I think I'm different, this existential thing works
In my class for a whole year and nothing and now

Things are moving, the cone and all and on the way back to the library
Can I see you again, maybe go to a movie? Sure she says
Here's my phone number, I live in Schenectady. Schenectady? I say
Yes, I commute to school; you can take a bus to pick me up

A bus trip from my Albany all the way to Schenectady—three miles away
She isn't on campus, she's a commuter student, she's different
And to get on a bus for a date—the new me isn't that new
I never really saw Karen again but that day in the park

I told her how I decided to meet her
All about Camus, Sartre, Existentialism and death
She seemed really uninterested
So existential

WHEN WE MEET

It's as if on
A swan led lake

A graceful God
Marks off

Land and sea
Takes the air

In his hand
Pillows it around us

Gives a gentle push
And for a time we glide

In wonder if heaven
Could be as sweet

ORBITING

I have not seen
The earth in blue
But for her eyes

Not touched
The China silk
But her breasts

Not lived the air
Of the Redwoods
But took her to bed

While the wind
Carried our story
To the stars

WHY DO LOVERS WHISPER?

Secrets to share but alone in bed?
What does a whisper say?

You whisper so the sparrow
Outside our window

Comes out of the cold
Perches on the sill

You whisper so the black cat
All mystery himself wonders

Is there something
Even I fail to know?

You whisper to hint to the lamb
Love does more than visit

You whisper to calm the tiger
Love finds a place to live

THE SWING AT ORIENT POINT

There on the beach a swing for two
and in the late afternoon empty

We sit and take in the world, we two
and words are said but not remembered

Something to pass the time
'How lovely, how perfect…'

But all that's needed is my foot
that sets the swing to swinging

And the folks years ago who said
Here, let's put a swing here

Just one, we'll make it strong
to survive the salt air

We'll make it for
one set of lovers, just one

We'll give them the autumn sky and sea
And time and death will disappear

LOVE AND THE BASTARD

I hate the bastard she said
But honey, he's your father

Mom he walked out on you
But he's your father

Walked out Mom, why? You don't know, do you?
He said he was unhappy

What does that mean, Mom? Nothing.
You don't really want to look, do you?

On those college teaching nights.
Remember how he dressed—all slicked up

For what? And those trips to the library
Endless trips to the library, Mom are you blind?

Honey, I love him
I see what I have to see

What love lets me see

PART II

VALENTINE'S DAY AT THE HOME

How's it going, Dad?
Ok, he says in his easy chair
Dressed neatly in clean shirt and sweater
He looks sharper than when Mom was alive

But you should see what they're doing today.
Took all the married and a few couples
You know the people that got together
They're giving them a party

Separate from the rest of us.
They moved my table and I had to eat lunch
All the way in the back.
For what, seven, maybe eight couples

They get the party and we get shit.
So it's not right? I said
Yes, and you see that guy across the hall.
Lenny, moved in last month

So I see Peggy from my table
Go into his room
I don't know if he's
Fucking her or not.

My Dad at 88
Finally I hear him link fucking to sex
Up to now getting fucked is what happens
To the little guy in this country

When I walk him to supper
We pass the party
Dad wears his 'I don't care' face
But I catch him peeking

ABOUT THE LIE OF DIVORCE

I remember when I bought Rose the blouse
V-neck... Native-American embroidery
Winter soft wool, a gift of the first
No...the second year of marriage
Oh, I loved her in it...I loved her then

I see the same blouse on a stranger
The Rose times come back and saying simply
"I'm divorced"—in the singles scene seems wrong
See I'm divorced except for this blouse
Divorced except when Sinatra sings 'Time after Time'
Divorced except for the two daughters
As beautiful as she was...is

My friend says *So the divorce...a mistake?*
And I say *No*

Look, I'm on the sandlot and I chase a ball
Crash into a hedge, branches up my nose
Bloodied lips and cheeks
Funny to others and anger for me
Divorce the game...no way

Later, I'm in center field—summer breeze
Another hit...a good one...and I run hard...run sweet
And I...the ball meet and it is as Rose in that blouse
The moment...the moment...the sweet moment

MY FEMININE SIDE

Dear diary
Never got a chance as a teen to confess so I hope it's not too late
You know I like to cry, especially at movies even those with Arnold
Women say they love men who show their feelings
But although they will hold my hand for a time
Deep inside I hear them thinking *Weak little shit*

Then there's Maggie and the very warm first night
But two months later trouble
Seems I cover my mouth with my hand as I talk
She reached across the table pulled it down said speak up
Wow, diary someone who really needs to run the ship

So it almost ended until she called and said
Well, it's over but we can still be fuck buddies
You know from Sex and the City
Best thing we do is sex so why not just that?
Dear diary sounded good to me

So I call and Maggie says fine eight o'clock in the city
"But wait, how about dinner?" "No" she says
"Are you sure?" I say "Yes," she says
Well, diary at the diner I ate alone and it felt strange

Grilled chicken sandwich no help
Left me to stare at an empty place setting
But at eight o'clock I show up and boom we are in bed
And boom we are out of bed And boom I am home
And boom it's really over And I think Oh no, my god

It's me that wants the flowers, candlelight, sipping of the wine
Dear diary that night I gobbled two pints of Haagen Daz chocolate
Watched Oprah late a program on why men don't understand
I began to cry because finally I understood every word

IN HER BEDROOM

Stare at me, will you, gray photograph of the stone
Stare at me naked in her bed

Watch me dress, begin with my watch
You won't forget it, if you put it in your shoe she said

Was it eight years ago, the last time?
And Ansel Adams, my friend, are you still on the wall?

In your cold beauty, Yosemite, isn't it?
She told me she had spent time in your West

I understood that part, but with the days and nights
Your grays filled that room

I wonder has she told those who followed about the incest—father
Then brother? Funny, how I cling to anything to stay special

Came here, looked up and that first time
Not the soft colors I expected, instead your stark tones of gray

What chance my petty warmth before your mountain of stone?
Lover bring your heat but soon the cold will come

Kill the child in you
Oh, I am going on

Talking to this picture on the wall means nothing
Same as the loving I did there means nothing

But if you are still on that wall
Could you give me a call

When she decides
To take you down?

MY RED DRESS

Hottest item in my closet
What does this male wear?
Look at her in that red dress
Check out that cling—those curves
Well, buddy what about us?
Is it the package between the legs?
First time I heard a lover say
Oh, I knew about your size
I wondered how? Pants too tight?
The same lover talked about butts
Mockingly about my friend Clark
He has no butt she said
I think what could he wear? Football pads?

So easy for a woman, a bit of cleavage
Even pretend push me up cleavage
A peek of skin at the shoulder
A sliver at the back
We men helplessly stand at attention.
Forced to ask what do we strive for?

My god, we have no red dress
No easy call to the wild
And I forgot their shoes
Everyone of them has
At least one pair
Steal a glance in that closet
There they are
Fuck me pumps

Ever hear of a fuck me loafer?
A fuck me shirt and tie?
Where's my red dress?
Where's my fuck me pumps?
Women, you lucky bunch you

I DON'T KNOW

Look at any Match. com profile
And every woman knows what she wants
Honesty, a friend, sense of humor...on and on
No sense of doubt—not a hint

I thought I gave them what they said they needed
Honesty, funny, slow walks in the park all that stuff
And things didn't work out—left me full of doubt about them
About myself—meanwhile the sketches stayed the same

But then just a month ago, here's Crystal
Her profile—not sure of the kind of guy she's looking for
On the phone I say *You're not sure?* She says *I hate to admit it but yes*
That first meeting at Starbucks I decide to test her

Tall, grande, venti?
She says *I don't know*—*Yes,* I shout
We rush into each other's arms
Swoon to the coffee shop floor

At her place just before bed
I say—*Your favorite position?*
She says *I don't know*
Yes... we go at it

After I ask *Was it good for you?*
She says *I don't know*
And I think
Damn, I'm in love

DELIOS

The Greek tour boat landed on the island where a herdsman
And twenty-two sheep stood crunched at the edge of the dock.

Wendy and I left to wander the ruins, our path fresh and brave
Through the brambles and bushes that tore at our legs.

Lovers at midlife playing child games
We moved to a home buried, beneath the land

Counted the rooms, hid behind the pillars and peed
Just outside the walls as if polite guests of these ancient folk.

Then the time came to do as other tourists do, climb the only hill
Buy the T-shirt, and fiddle with the trinkets.

But that house left us in wonder at how the world
Had spun us together for a time and said

Here, souls, a place where others lived, shared, and died
Come take some breaths as well

We give you these stones as our lives.

ELVIS AT THE DUNKIN DONUTS

Coffee at hand I sit alone and begin
To read some Walt Whitman

A bearded dark skinned fellow stops before me
His look seen time and again in all the media

Syria, Iraq, Iran, Pakistan, Ukraine
He asks **What are you reading?**

I look up and push away Syria, Iraq, all of them and say
It's Walt Whitman and read aloud

'For every atom belonging to me
As good belongs to you'

He smiles offers a hand to shake and says
I'm Elvis and that's good what you read

I nod and and he takes a seat opposite
He goes on **That's true what you read**

I hear about his 13 hour workdays and rotten employers
And after 20 minutes or so he heads towards the door

Turns says **I stop you from reading and you talk to me**
Our atoms are joining

SUBWAY EYES

The fellow offers Sue his seat and she refuses with a *Thank you*
She looks at me troubled and asks without a word

Do I look that old? and I smile and say nothing
Think of my last look in the mirror and the thought

My Sue gets in bed with this creature aged with crevasses
Think of the change that comes with me on the street

Free of reflective surfaces and living inside
As a handsome 35 year old ready to play seducer

There's the easy part but comes the lover Sue
The grandma and the mark that her beauty rests

Deep in my mind—real as any fashion in the window
I give her that and greet her with *Beautiful*

And she says with a smile *No…not so*
I smile back to say I see what my heart sees

SEXUALLY ACTIVE

The young doctor asks the senior *Are you still sexually active?*
Yes…yes… Sue answers
The doctor says *Wow, there's hope for me as I age*
Yes…oh yes her patient almost whispers

Told the story I think how some see age
The thoughtful slower moving senior
Taken to be cautious…soft
Easygoing…laid back…not quite dead but almost

When I ask Sue about the doctor she says
Next one who asks I'll say
If you must know, look I'm 66
And fucking quite well

SMALL TALK

In bed I check my watch, 6 a.m., too early to begin the story of morning
But as I turn to catch a few more minutes of snooze she says *What time
   is it?*

Oh, she's awake and I say *Six* and ask *Good sleep?* Hear *Yes*
I don't know what came next—patter about kids, shows, what we're
   reading

It goes on…no strain…no search for what to say until I check my watch
Hey, it's seven I say Hear *We better get up*

Tell of losing an hour and the world says ' So what?"
A little island of life in this bed, c'mon give us a tale

The winter cold outside forces a fragile everywhere
But anyone looking sees comfort here

Two lying side by side
My breaths…her breaths…bits of this and that

Time to let the light in
The hour lost in unseen sweetness

THE SWERVE

Lucretius explained it
Atoms never die

But couple then uncouple
Tied then liberated

What survives? *Love, only love*
Lucretius says *Let the lover go*

The beloved always slips away
We only borrow these ties

My cousin the gun in his mouth and then...
The swerve... oh Lucretius...the swerve

The mourners come to his ashes
Try to understand but

Clarity lies with the atoms
They say *We're off to be reborn*

Hear us...we're off
And beside the urn—photos

Atoms in place...ours for a time
And we cry...we loved these atoms

Stay...come back
Even as they remind us

Some day the swerve will be ours
We...cousins to the stars

THERE ARE SKIES THAT ARE CLOSER TO THE TRUTH

You know the ones I mean
The sun plays peek-a-boo
Clouds at a rage—half torn

Tells that the flesh and blood
That so needs flesh and blood
Knows in helpless wonder

How a heart torn apart
Might be saved by
One move of earth

Look here, a lover's tears
That stir—a gift
Embrace it

AS A KISS

Summer heat
Six years old
Walk with Grandma
From the village
To Central Park
Cheeks flushed pink

A stream
Skirting about the stones
Children splashing
Mothers
Soaking their feet

I reach between the rocks
In tiny hands cup the flow
Draw it to my lips
Cool spills
Everywhere

BAFFLING

My plans to speak
Of the love I feel

After a hello kiss, small talk, a movie…
At dinner I take in her look

Her glow and say *Beautiful*
Ready to go on, when Sue with a smile

Points a finger across her lips
I say *You continue to baffle me*

Sue still smiling takes one…two breaths
It's ok you know

There's courage in remaining baffled
I sigh into silence—think

Love doesn't make life perfect
Just makes it come alive

Greg Moglia's poems have been published in over 300 journals in the U.S., Canada, England, Australia, India, Sweden, Austria and Belguim including *Southern Humanities Review, Rattle, William and Mary Review, Wisconsin Review, Paterson Literary Review* and *Peregrine*. He is an eight—time winner of an Allan Ginsberg Poetry Award and his poem "Why Do Lovers Whisper" was nominated for a Pushcart Prize.

Professor Moglia holds a doctorate from NYU in Philosophy of Science Education. He spent 37 years as a teacher of high school physics and psychology concurrent with 27 years of teaching Philosophy of Education at NYU. Dr. Moglia is now a full-time poet writing about the foibles of mid-life dating, the challenge of aging parents, the sweetness of lovers both old and new.

www.ingramcontent.com/pod-product-compliance
Lightning Source LLC
LaVergne TN
LVHW041602070426
835507LV00011B/1249